O N E
With
G O D

Author of

One with God: A Tool for Development,
Volume 2
and

One with God: A Tool for Understanding and
Practical Application of One With God,
Volume 3

ONE

With

GOD

Volume 1

Joseph Everette Williams Jr

JASSAI Publishing
United States

JASSAI Publishing
PO Box 32909
Detroit MI 48232-0909

One With God: Volume 1—Copyright © 2022 by Joseph Everette Williams Jr., JASSAI Publishing, a Michigan Company

For special discounts on bulk purchases, please contact JASSAI Publishing at themeplaceinstitute@gmail.com.

Interior Design by JASSAI Publishing
Cover Design by JASSAI Publishing Copyright © 2022

Published in Detroit, Michigan, by JASSAI Publishing

Library of Congress Cataloguing-in-Publication Data

Williams, Joseph Everett Jr.

One With God Vol 1:
/Joseph Everette Williams Jr.
p. cm.
ISBN 978-0-9897074-5-9

Printed in the United States of America

Requests for information should be addressed to:
Jassai Publishing
PO Box 32909
Detroit MI 48232.0909
showersblessings@gmail.com

[Tis title is also available as an e-book]

Contents

INTRODUCTION

I would ask the reader to hold all judgement of this work and title until every word is read. This is my only instruction. In doing so, it should develop one feeling or thought after another. I have not tried to use neutral gender in this writing, nor have I tried to use him or her. I left this up to the reader to make that designation as they deem appropriate.

These are little distinctions the average person may overlook in the process to become the above-average person. These distinctions can make all the difference if used. They are disarmingly simple, but indeed powerful.

Know. Apply. Will. Be. Do Have!

G O D

The Thought of God creating itself and then creating everything else. We are a part of that Word. If we operate our lives from that essence, that center, we have everything. We have the power to direct the unlimited power of God…

Reflect. Write.

_____

_____

_____

_____

_____

_____

_____

_____

_____

ONE WITH GOD

POWER

We have the Power to direct the unlimited Power of God. We are One with and a part of the Power—God! We have everything we need to have health, wealth and long life...

Reflect. Write.

_____

_____

_____

_____

_____

_____

_____

_____

_____

IDEA

The Idea. The Thought. The Word of God created itself and then created everything else. We are a part of that Word. We are one with God. We have everything.

Reflect. Write.

_____

_____

_____

_____

_____

_____

_____

_____

_____

You

We are One with God.

One shared center with that Essence of God. One shared center with the Thought of God. One shared center with the Word of God.

One shared center with that Idea. One shared center with that Power. One shared center with that Force. One shared center with that Energy. One shared center with God.

Reflect. Write.

_____

_____

_____

CENTER

Being (Be) One with God. If we operate our lives as part of that Center, that essence, we have everything. We have the power to direct the unlimited power of God. We are one with God...

Reflect. Write.

_____

_____

_____

_____

_____

_____

_____

_____

_____

EVERYTHING

One with God. In oneness with God, we have the power to be, do, and have anything we desire. We have the unlimited power of God inside of us to have health, wealth, and long life.

Reflect. Write.

_____

_____

_____

_____

_____

_____

_____

_____

JOSEPH EVERETTE WILLIAMS JR

October 28, 2015

Mr. Joseph E. Williams, Jr.
Vicksburg, Mississippi

Dear Joseph:

Thank you for writing. There is no denying that even with the significant progress we have made as a country over the past several decades, painful aspects of our Nation's history continue to cast a long shadow with regard to race relations and our communities. Important work still lies ahead, and we all have roles to play.

Too many communities continue to battle chronic poverty, unemployment, isolation, and a basic lack of opportunity. These problems have consequences that reverberate through our society and the lives of individual families. It is up to each of us to lead in our communities and to ensure that all levels of government are working to revitalize our neighborhoods, improve our schools, and ensure that success in this country is only dependent on the dreams and will of our people, not the zip codes they are born into. By recognizing our common humanity and treating every person as important, we can make opportunity real for all Americans.

We started the *My Brother's Keeper* initiative to address persistent opportunity gaps and tear down barriers that too often prevent our young people, including boys and young men of color, from realizing their full potential. Additionally, my Task Force on 21st Century Policing put forward 59 concrete recommendations on how we can build better trust and respect between communities and law enforcement officers, and we are engaged with cities and towns across America to encourage them to put these proposals into practice. And we continue to fight to build a smarter, fairer, and more effective criminal justice system in our communities, courtrooms, and cell blocks.

Solving these problems will take sustained effort from all of us, and they won't be fixed if we only pay attention when tragedy strikes. Change depends on our actions, our attitudes, and the things we teach our children every day. If each of us makes an effort—no matter how hard it may sometimes seem—consciences can be stirred, consensus can be built, and change can be realized.

Again, thank you for writing. There's nothing our country can't handle if we look squarely at the problem, and there is no greater form of patriotism than championing the belief that America is not yet finished and a brighter future lies ahead. I hope you will continue to commit both thought and action toward the solutions needed in your community.

Sincerely,

2820 E Main Street
Vicksburg, MS 39183-2426
Email: rockettaxicab@aol.com
Phone: (601) 636-0491

JOSEPH E. Williams, Jr.

December 8, 2015

President Barack H. Obama
The White House
1600 Pennsylvania Ave NW
Washington, DC 20500-0003

Re: October 28, 2015 Letter and Subsequent email on the Syrian Refugee Crisis

Dear Mr. President:

Would every man/woman go to heaven because of the love of Jesus Christ?
But if the only reason you make it to heaven is the fear of hell, you made it to heaven anyway.

You cannot be a Muslim unless you believe in Jesus (peace and blessings be on all the men and women of God). That includes you. The nineteen (19) Surah (Chapter) of the Qur'an is entitled "Mary the Mother of Jesus" (Maryam). There is not a Surah or Chapter entitled Mohammad.

I would entitle this letter, "Three Brothers Fighting Over the Way and the Method to the Father," the physical father and the spiritual father. Every man has the right to find his own way. I have that right and I take that right.

In the beginning there was one flock and one fold so shall it be in the end. Abraham had a wife named Sarah and she was barren. She told Abraham to take her handmaid Haggar and they conceived a son Ishmael. Now after many years had passed, Sarah was advised that she would have a son.

What is now a dispute over land, oil, money, and blood feud between the Arabs and the Jews, started out over the right of the first born over the legitimacy or illegitimacy of the sons of

2820 E Main Street
Vicksburg, MS 39183-2426
Email: rockettaxicab@aol.com
Phone: (601) 636-0491

Abraham. Should the promised child Isaac get the first born rights or should his older brother Ishmael? This is where you get the split between the Arabs and the Jews.

We move on to Isaac who begot Jacob who had twelve sons, who became the head of the twelve tribes of Israel. Each son led a tribe, Reuben, Simeon, Levi, Judah, Dan, Naphtali, Gad, Asher, Issachar, Zebulun, Joseph and Benjamin. From the tribe of Judah you get the line of David (King David, the first King) that is the initial line of Jesus Christ.

The feud between the Christian and Jewish belief system was over the legitimacy or illegitimacy of the person of Jesus Christ. Was he the son of God or was he the son of Joseph? Consider three brothers; a Muslim, a Christian and a Jew with the same physical father Abraham and the same spiritual father God fighting over the way, and the method to the physical and spiritual father. All three are physical brothers with Abraham as the father of their religion (Muslim, Christian, Jewish). All believe in one God. They call him by different names due to language differences. Muslims call him Allah, Jews call him Yahweh and Christians call him God. He is one and so is Abraham.

What have we done as brothers? Again we have divided ourselves into Baptist, Methodist, Catholics, etc. Our religious practices have divided us again as Sunni, Shiites, Hasballah, the American Muslims and the Nation of Islam. Within the Jewish religion we have the Orthodox Jews, we have the Jews that believes in Jesus and those that do not.

God is one and so are we, we are one with God and we are one with Abraham. We are all Allah. We are all Abraham. We are all Yahweh. Jesus said it this way, physically he was from the tribe of Judah the line of David but by the spirit he was from the spirit of God. David said it this way, "Ye are all Gods sons and daughters of the most high God." When looking at the Lord's Prayer, we say, "Our father" not his father, not your father, not their father. Jesus said you understand these things in the physical, why do you have so much trouble understanding it in the spiritual?

Jesus said do not worship me but worship the father but follow my example (behavior) and greater things you will do that I have done.

"The blood of Abraham, God father of the chosen people, still flow in the veins of Arabs, Jews and Christians. Too much of it has been spilled in grasping for the inheritance of the revered patriarch in the Middle East." (Abraham).....Jimmie Carter

ONE WITH GOD

2820 E Main Street
Vicksburg, MS 39183-2426
Email: rockettaxicab@aol.com
Phone: (601) 636-0491

The Bible said that when the first blood was shed among his children God asked Cain, the slayer, "Where is Abel, thy brother?" Cain replied, "I know not. Am I my brother's keeper?".....Genesis 4:8

Again thank you for writing, "There is nothing our country can't handle if we look squarely at the problem, there is no greater form of patriotism then challenging the belief that America is not yet finished and a brighter future lies ahead. I hope you will continue to commit both thought and action towards the solutions needed." (the United States of America)..... Barack Obama.

"I pray these words bring us together as brothers in fact and indeed."....Joseph E. Williams

Respectfully submitted,

Joseph Williams

Joseph E. Williams, Jr.

Cc: Loretta E. Lynch, Attorney General
        Michele Obama, First Lady
        Dr. Callaway

THE WHITE HOUSE

WASHINGTON

March 24, 2016

Mr. Joseph E. Williams, Jr.
Vicksburg, Mississippi

Dear Joseph:

Thank you for writing. I appreciate your taking the time to share your thoughts with me.

As a Christian, I believe faith can play a positive role in our politics. Faith helps us find the vision and strength to see the world we want to build. It reminds us to love and understand one another, and to treat with dignity and respect those with whom we share a brief moment on this earth. The particular faith that motivates each of us can bring us together to feed the hungry, comfort the afflicted, make peace where there is strife, and lift up those who have fallen on hard times.

Faith may also bring us to different conclusions about the issues we face, but these honest disagreements need not divide us. America is strong because of our diversity, our openness, and the way we respect every faith, and we must reject any politics that targets people because of race or religion.

I created the White House Office of Faith-Based and Neighborhood Partnerships to support organizations that work on behalf of our communities. Whether it is a secular group advising families facing foreclosure or a faith-based organization providing job training to the unemployed, these groups are helping Americans across the country. This office strives to better our Nation without blurring the line our Founders wisely drew between church and state.

Our Nation's proud tradition of religious tolerance and diversity is firmly rooted in our founding documents. I honor these principles, and will continue—as many Presidents have before me—to partner with people of faith to care for our neighbors and strengthen our ties to one another.

Please stay in touch by visiting www.WhiteHouse.gov. Thank you, again, for writing

Sincerely,

38

CONCLUSION

How?

We have the ability to direct the unlimited power of God.

- By recognizing it.
- By learning to transform your mind to be in alignment with God's power. How?
- By repeating your aims, desires, and goals, when you go to bed and again when you wake up. In this way, the unlimited power of God is directed to transform the mind to accomplish your aims, desires, and goals, by practical means! In essence, to bring them into reality with the one-ness of God's reality. With this method, you are empowered to create your reality, condition, and environment. How? It is an easy, effortless, fast process to achieve health, wealth, and long life one with God.

1. Recognize you have the inherent power of God to direct the unlimited power of God.
2. Learn to direct it, use, and apply that power through mind science to produce your desired results, reality, and conditions.
3. Review goals, aims, and desires every day before you go to sleep and when you wake up.
4. This puts "Cosmic Habit-Force", the 17 Laws of Success working for you. Cosmic force is the unifying agent that

acts as a magnet to draw the ideas, things, and people to aid in the accomplishment of your aims, One with God...

Reflect. Write.

_____

_____

_____

_____

_____

_____

_____

_____

_____

_____

_____

_____

JOSEPH EVERETTE WILLIAMS JR

Afterthought 1

You encompass everything to be, do, and have. You must learn oneness with God. Be it. Do It. Have It. Keep It. Use It.

Reflect. Write.

_____

_____

_____

_____

_____

_____

_____

_____

_____

AFTERTHOUGHT 2

This power, force, and energy the Bible calls God is first presented in Genesis. It starts the creative work of creation that never stops, that never ends, and that is a continual evolution in all of us.

Reflect. Write.

_____

_____

_____

_____

_____

_____

_____

_____

AFTERTHOUGHT 3

The soul is the breath of life. The breath of life comes from God. The breath comes in from God at birth, then goes back to God at death, from eternity to eternity.

Reflect. Write.

_____

_____

_____

_____

_____

_____

_____

_____

_____

AFTERTHOUGHT 4

Existence exists. The thought. The word. The idea is the existence that exist. In the Beginning was the Word, the Word was with God, the Word was God! We are one with God.

Reflect. Write.

_____

_____

_____

_____

_____

_____

_____

_____

JOSEPH EVERETTE WILLIAMS JR

AFTERTHOUGHT 5

The love of life is sexual love.
The motivation for love is for physical pleasure.
The purpose of love is for future generations.
Love is the will to life for future, generations, nations and/or individuals.

Reflect. Write.

_____

_____

_____

_____

_____

_____

_____

_____

ONE WITH GOD

61

THE BEGINNING

Reflect. Write.

_____

_____

_____

_____

_____

_____

_____

_____

_____

_____

_____

_____

SUGGESTED READINGS

Psalms 91, King James Version

The Edinburgh and Dore Lectures on Mental Science by: Thomas Troward

The Creative Process in the Individual by Thomas Troward

Bible Meaning and Bible Mystery by Thomas Troward

The Laws of Success by Napoleon Hill

Psalms 27, King James Version

Psalms 82, King James Version

Atom Smashing Power of the Mind by Charles Fillmore

PROPOSAL CONTRACT FOR PERSONAL WORKSHOPS BY THE AUTHOR

1. Travel Cost:
   a. Airfare roundtrip/rent-a-car fees. Under 100 mile radius or less will drive.
   b. Transportation from and back to the airport from site as appropriate.
   c. Meals and hotel for one night.

2. All fees/transportation paid in advance.
3. The organization/individual can provide some or all of these services to defer cost.
4. Author's contact information: everetteJoseph54@gmail.com

TESTIMONIALS

Following your reading of One With God, you will be equipped with the knowledge that will afford you a more thorough and rewarding understanding of your true identity that is found in your Oneness with God.

Mavis Randall, Educator, Vicksburg Public Schools

A STATEMENT OF PROFESSIONAL EXPERIENCES BY JOSEPH WILLIAMS JR.

I grew up in a small community in rural Mississippi, the fifth of seven children. I attended the neighborhood grade school and high school. I was the first black male graduate from Saint Aloysius High School in 1971. The student population was 300 whites, five blacks, two of whom being my brothers. I was caught up in the integration issues of the 1960's, which sparked my interest in higher education.

I was selected as one of the Outstanding Young Men in America, given by the National Jaycees. I was the first black Graduate Assistant in the Behavioral Science Department of Delta State University, Cleveland, Miss., from 1978-1979. During this time, I earned a master's degree in Guidance and Counseling, while employed as Residence Counselor at Mississippi Valley State University, Itta Bena, Miss.

Throughout my life, I have had many practical experiences in living, resulting in my ability to evaluate myself and developing self-confidence which complements my outgoing personality. I have some understanding and great appreciation for those things that make people human and believe that the pursuit of knowledge should continue throughout life. Therefore, I was inspired to write this little book.

Outline for Workshop Presentation for One With God

We have to build a better man before we can build a better world. –Anonymous

1. We will speak in part and detail only to explain, only for understanding. But we must always think, oneness, wholeness, one with God. We must not get lost in the details.
2. What we will talk about can be found in Psalm 27, 28 and 91. The very root of our talk is "as a man thinks so is he," think one with God, made in his image and likeness, both man and woman.
3. Let that mind be in you that was in whom? What mind was that? The mind of God! In the book of Psalm, we read, "You are all God's sons and daughters of the most high God." Let that be the starting point, the rules of engagement for this presentation.
4. Have you read the book?
5. Question/testimonials from the readers (presentation by the author).

www.ingramcontent.com/pod-product-compliance
Lightning Source LLC
Chambersburg PA
CBHW071020040426
42443CB00007B/874